Keyword Tracker

Designed by
TeeCee Design Studio

Keyword Tracker

Keyword Tracker

Keyword Tracker

Keyword Tracker

Keyword Tracker

Keyword Tracker

Keyword Tracker

Keyword Tracker

Keyword Tracker

Keyword Tracker

Keyword Tracker

Keyword Tracker

Keyword Tracker

Keyword Tracker

Keyword Tracker

Keyword Tracker

Keyword Tracker

Keyword Tracker

Keyword Tracker

Keyword Tracker

Keyword Tracker

Keyword Tracker

Keyword Tracker

Keyword Tracker

Keyword Tracker

Keyword Tracker

Keyword Tracker

Keyword Tracker

Keyword Tracker

Keyword Tracker

Keyword Tracker

Keyword Tracker

Keyword Tracker

Keyword Tracker

Keyword Tracker

Keyword Tracker

Keyword Tracker

Keyword Tracker

Keyword Tracker

Keyword Tracker

Keyword Tracker

Keyword Tracker

Keyword Tracker

Keyword Tracker

Keyword Tracker

Keyword Tracker

Keyword Tracker

Keyword Tracker

Keyword Tracker

Keyword Tracker

Keyword Tracker

Keyword Tracker

Keyword Tracker

Keyword Tracker

Keyword Tracker

Keyword Tracker

Keyword Tracker

Keyword Tracker

Keyword Tracker

Keyword Tracker

Keyword Tracker

Keyword Tracker

Keyword Tracker

Keyword Tracker

Keyword Tracker

Keyword Tracker

Keyword Tracker

Keyword Tracker

Keyword Tracker

Keyword Tracker

Keyword Tracker

Keyword Tracker

Keyword Tracker

Keyword Tracker

Keyword Tracker

Keyword Tracker

Keyword Tracker

Keyword Tracker

Keyword Tracker

Keyword Tracker

Keyword Tracker

Keyword Tracker

Keyword Tracker

Keyword Tracker

Keyword Tracker

Keyword Tracker

Keyword Tracker

Keyword Tracker

Keyword Tracker

Keyword Tracker

Keyword Tracker

Keyword Tracker

Keyword Tracker

Keyword Tracker

Keyword Tracker

Keyword Tracker

Keyword Tracker

Keyword Tracker

Thank you so much for your purchase.

I really do hope that this book has helped you,
even in some small way.

Would you like to see different designs/styles?

I am always very happy to hear from customers,
so please feel free to email me on

teeceedesignstudio@yahoo.com